THE TABLETOP LEARNING SERIES

RAINBOW FUN

Rainbows to Keep, Share, and Give Away
by Imogene Forte

Incentive Publications, Inc.
Nashville, Tennessee

Illustrated by Marta Zellars
Cover illustration by Becky Cutler
Edited by Sally Sharpe

Library of Congress Catalog Number 86-82873
ISBN 0-86530-161-1

Copyright © 1987 by Incentive Publications, Inc., Nashville, Tennessee. All rights reserved. No part of this publication may be reproduced, stored in a retrieval system, or transmitted in any way or by any means (electronic, mechanical, photocopying, recording, or otherwise) without prior written permission from Incentive Publications, Inc.
THE TABLETOP LEARNING SERIES™ is a trademark of Incentive Publications, Inc., Nashville, TN 37215

THIS RAINBOW BOOK BELONGS TO

_____

CONTENTS

ix   A Note to Kids

RAINBOW CRAFTS
12   Blow a Rainbow
14   Rainbow Candles
16   Rainbow Pudding Paint
18   Rainbow Place Mats
19   A String-Along Rainbow
20   Rainbow Friendship Book
21   A Rainbow Surprise Box
22   Rainbow Rainwear
24   Rainbow Feelings
26   Mark Your Place With a Rainbow
27   Twin Rainbows

RAINBOW FUN
30   Rainbow Crossword
32   Rainbow Ring-Around
34   Rainbow Expressions
36   Rainbow Riddles
38   Color A True Rainbow
40   Rainbow Hide-N-Seek

41 "Rain Bows"
42 Somewhere Over the Rainbow
44 Raindrop Prisms
45 Sole-O-Rainbow
46 Rainbow Award
48 Rainbow Sneakers
49 Spin a Rainbow
50 Rainbow Fruit Bowl
52 A Rainbow to Remember
54 Has Anybody Seen a Rainbow?
55 Rainbow Pencil Toppers

RAINBOW RECIPES
58 Meet Professor Roy G. Biv
60 Rainbow Bubbles
61 Dough Your Own Rainbow
62 Shake a Sandy Rainbow
64 Rainbow Cubes
65 Rainbow Reflections
66 Rainbow Popsicles
68 Rainbow Cookies
70 Rainbow Patterns
72 File Your Rainbows
74 One Dozen and One Make-and-Take Rainbows

78 ANSWER KEY
79 INDEX

A NOTE TO KIDS

Boxes and bags, paper plates and cups, yarn, ribbon and string... all of these very ordinary things can be turned into extraordinary rainbows. All you have to do is use your imagination!

This book has been written to give you some fun ideas for things to make and do with the marvelous "junk" that is already at your finger tips. All of the projects, games and activities are easy to make and use. Some are just for you. Others are group projects which will involve a friend or two.

After you have finished this book, you will have rainbows to keep, rainbows to share, and rainbows to give away. Some of the rainbows will be useful, and some will be just for fun!

So thumb through the book, choose a rainbow page, and see what you can make!

Imogene Forte

BLOW A RAINBOW

WHAT TO USE:
- rainbow colors of thin tempera paint
- drinking straws
- large sheet of white construction or shelf paper
- sheet of blue construction paper
- newspapers
- scissors
- glue

WHAT TO DO:
1. Spread newspapers over the working surface.
2. Place the white paper on the newspaper surface.
3. Spill two or three large drops of one color of paint on the white paper.
4. Blow through the straw to spread the paint on the paper. Turn the paper as you blow to make interesting designs.
5. Let the paint dry for a few minutes, and then spill two or three drops of another color.
6. Continue dropping and blowing colors of paint until your design is complete.
7. After the paint has dried, cut out a rainbow shape and glue it to a sheet of blue construction paper.

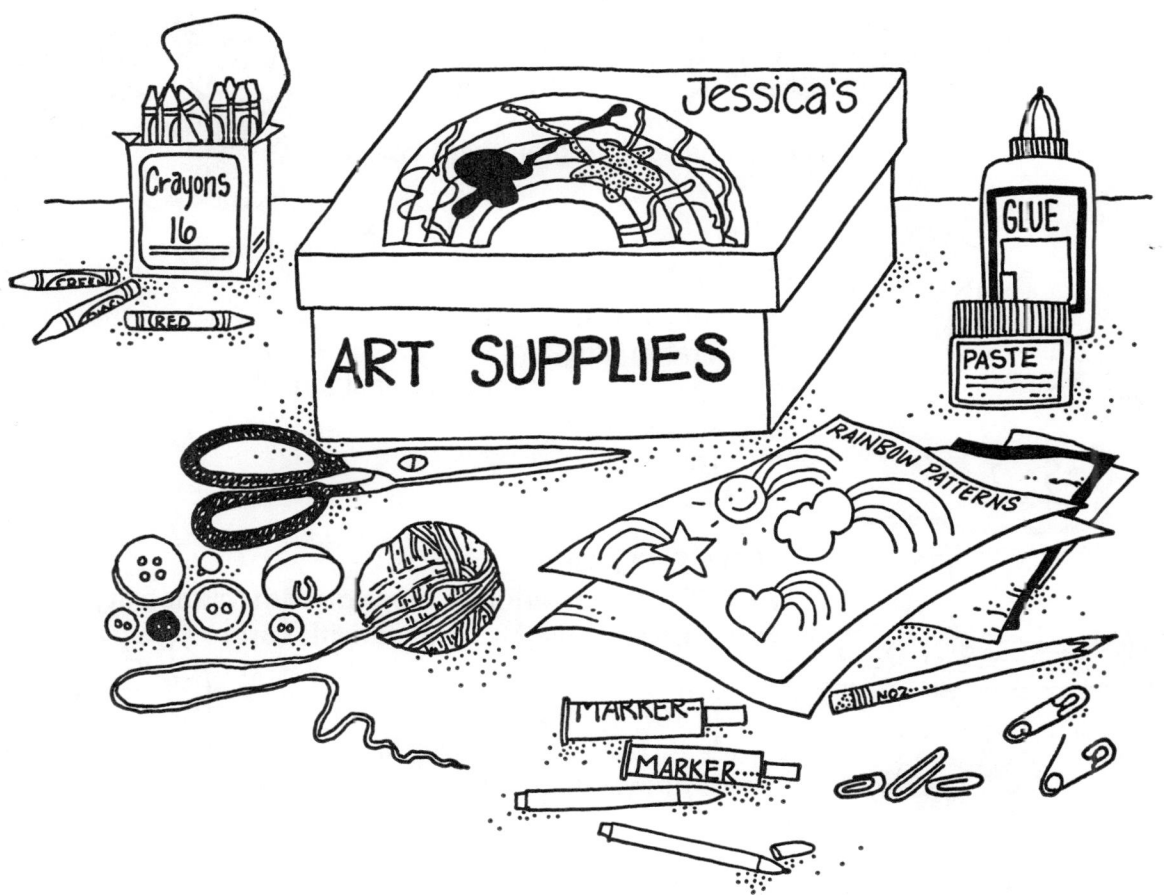

WHAT IS FUN:
Instead of gluing your rainbow design to a sheet of blue paper, glue your rainbow to the top of a white gift box to make a container for "rainbow" art supplies!

RAINBOW CANDLES

this candle is sure to glow with color!

WHAT TO USE:
- pint-sized milk carton
- paraffin block
- old wax crayons (use at least 3 rainbow colors)
- double boiler
- string
- scissors

WHAT TO DO:
FIRST -- ask an adult to help you with this activity. Hot paraffin must be handled with care!

1. Melt 1/3 of the paraffin block in a double boiler.

2. Add wax crayons to the melted paraffin. (Remember to remove the paper from the crayons!) Melt enough crayons to obtain the desired shade.

3. Wash and dry the milk carton. Cut the top off as shown.

4. Make a tiny slit in the bottom of the carton. Run a string through the hole and knot the string under the carton to make a wick.

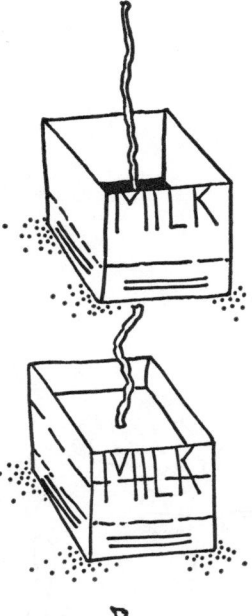

5. Pour the first rainbow color into the carton and let it harden. (Be sure to hold the string upright as you pour in the wax.)

6. Melt and pour the other rainbow colors, one at a time, in the same manner. Remember to let each layer harden before pouring another one!

7. When the candle has completely hardened, peel off the carton. (Putting the carton in cold water will make this easier.)

RAINBOW PUDDING PAINT

*lick and paint, paint and lick --
it's so much fun to do,
paint a rainbow pudding pix --
for a friend or just for you!*

WHAT TO USE:
- instant vanilla pudding
- food coloring (red, yellow, green, blue)
- 7 paper cups

HOW TO GET READY:
1. Make the instant vanilla pudding according to the directions on the box.
2. Evenly distribute the pudding in 7 cups.
3. To make the 7 colors of the rainbow, add food coloring to each cup of pudding and stir the mixture with a spoon. Follow this guide: cup 1 - red; cup 2 - orange (yellow and a touch of red); cup 3 - yellow; cup 4 - green; cup 5 - blue; cup 6 - indigo (lots of blue for a deep shade); cup 7 - violet (blue and a touch of red).
4. Spread newspapers over the work surface for an easy cleanup.
5. Lay finger painting paper or slick, white shelf paper over the newspaper.
6. Wash your hands and get ready to paint!

WHAT TO DO:
1. Paint rainbows with your pudding paint! Use spoons to drop the pudding paint on the paper and your hands to do the painting.
2. Paint a little -- lick a little. (Be careful not to eat too much!)
3. Paint rainbows as they really are by following the order of the colors in the picture, or design your own rainbows. Keep the colors separate, or mix them together for special effects. The sky is the limit!

RAINBOW PLACE MATS

WHAT TO USE:
- top of a cardboard box (about 12 x 18 inches with 1 inch sides)
- tape or glue
- markers and/or crayons
- scissors

WHAT TO DO:
1. Using crayons or markers, decorate the inside of the box top with lots of rainbows or with one rainbow in the background of an original scene.
2. Use paper cutouts and crayons or markers to complete the design or picture.
3. Choose a theme for your place mats to make them more special such as a seasonal or geometrical theme.
4. Make a rainbow place mat for yourself and for each member of your family!

WHAT IS FUN:
Plan a special meal for your family to use the rainbow place mats. Let each member try to find the place mat that you made for him or her. Cleanup will be easy -- the sides of the place mats keep the crumbs from scattering!

A STRING-ALONG RAINBOW

WHAT TO USE:
- cottage cheese or margarine container with lid
- glue
- yarn (each color of the rainbow)
- ball of string

WHAT TO DO:
1. Remove the lid from the container.
2. Cover the container and lid with glue.
3. Using one color at a time, wrap the yarn around the container to cover it. Do the same to the lid. (Press the cut end of each color of yarn firmly into the glue to hold it in place. Wipe away excess glue before starting the next color.)
4. Cut a hole in the center of the lid.
5. Put a ball of string in the container, replace the lid, and pull the loose end of string through the hole.

WHAT IS FUN:
Make a "string-along rainbow" for a Mother's Day, Father's Day, or birthday gift.

RAINBOW FRIENDSHIP BOOK

WHAT TO USE:
- construction paper
- yarn or string
- crayons or markers
- pen or pencil

WHAT TO DO:
1. Trace one of the rainbow patterns on pages 70 and 71, or draw your own rainbow on construction paper.
2. Use the pattern to trace rainbows of every color of the rainbow on construction paper. Cut out enough rainbows to make pages.
3. Draw lines on each rainbow to make 7 bands. Write a friend's name, address, and telephone number on each band.
4. Holding the rainbow pages together, punch 2 holes in the left side of the stack.
5. Run a piece of yarn or string through the holes and tie a bow to hold the book together. Make a cover for your rainbow book.

WHAT IS FUN:
Follow the directions above to make a rainbow autograph book. You'll have fun collecting the autographs of favorite friends and famous people!

A RAINBOW SURPRISE BOX

WHAT TO USE:
- big, sturdy box
- crepe paper in rainbow colors
- newspaper
- glue
- small boxes
- paper bags
- candy or little "surprises"

WHAT TO DO:
1. Glue strips of crepe paper on the big box to cover it.
2. Wrap candy or little surprises in small boxes or decorated paper bags. (Tie the paper bags with ribbon or yarn.)
3. Stuff the big box with balls of newspaper and hide the wrapped surprises in the box. As the guests leave your party, invite them to "dig in" and find a surprise to take home.

WHAT IS FUN:
Unwrapping the gifts will bring squeals of delight and giggles galore. What a fun way to end a party!

RAINBOW RAINWEAR

make your own designer fashions and stage a rainwear show!

WHAT TO USE:
- plastic garbage bags or clear dry cleaning bags
- scissors
- string

WHAT TO DO:
1. Cut, wrap, and tie the plastic bags to fashion your own rainwear.
2. Make coats, gloves, boots and hats with the bags for a fully rainproof outfit!

WHAT IS FUN:
Stage a rainwear fashion show with your friends. Let each friend model a rain creation and then talk about it. You might like to give all the parents tickets and invite them to this exclusive show!

RAINBOW FEELINGS

experiment with colors to express how you feel

WHAT TO USE:
- music (record, tape or radio)
- tempera paint: red, yellow, blue
- paintbrushes
- white paper
- newspapers

WHAT TO DO:
1. Spread newspapers over the work area.
2. Put white paper on the newspaper surface.
3. Turn on the music and paint with the colors you *feel*! (See the color chart on page 58 for mixing colors.)

Red + Yellow = Orange

*feel what you paint and paint what you feel,
look inside the colors to see what they reveal!*

MARK YOUR PLACE WITH A RAINBOW

*think how great this rainbow will look --
when holding your place in a favorite book!*

WHAT TO USE:
- white construction paper
- markers and/or crayons
- scissors
- glue

WHAT TO DO:
1. Cut out a rainbow-shaped bookmark from white construction paper.
2. Use crayons and/or markers to decorate the bookmark.
3. Cut a slit in the side of the rainbow so that the bookmark will fit over the edge of the page you want to hold.

WHAT IS FUN:
After making your own bookmark, make one for a friend who likes rainbows as much as you do!

TWIN RAINBOWS

WHAT TO USE:
- 2 sheets of heavy white paper
- sponge
- pan of water
- scissors
- crepe paper (several rainbow colors)

WHAT TO DO:
1. Put one sheet of white paper on a flat surface.
2. Cut strips of crepe paper to make a rainbow.
3. Wet the white paper thoroughly with a damp sponge.
4. Place the crepe paper strips on the white paper to form a rainbow.
5. Quickly cover the rainbow with a second sheet of white paper. Smooth the paper with your hands, making sure all sides are pressed together tightly.
6. Continue to rub over the surface of the paper, pressing down as you go.
7. Carefully remove the top paper and the crepe paper. You've made not one beautiful rainbow, but two!

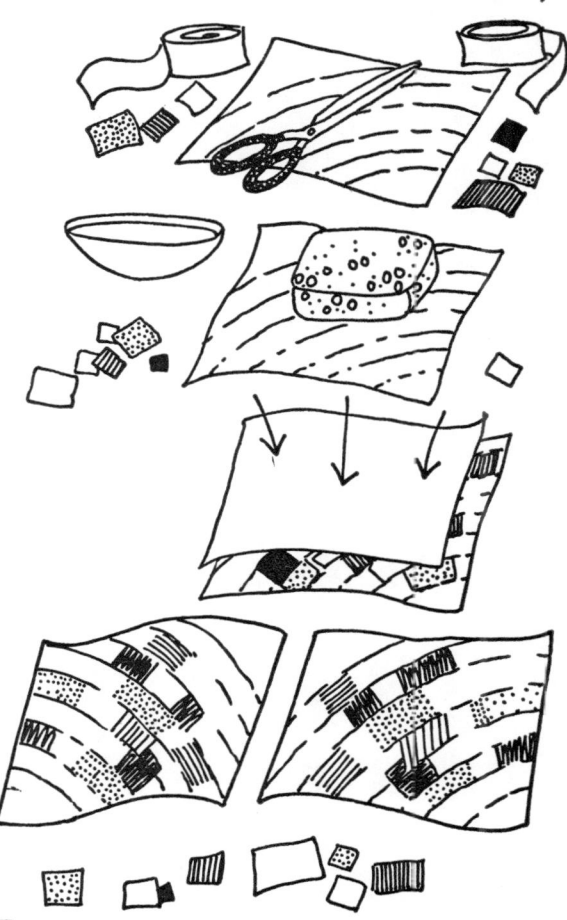

RAINBOW CROSSWORD

rainbow fun for a rainy day!

DOWN

2. _____ is soft water which contains little mineral matter.
3. The amount of water that falls in the form of rain, snow, etc. is called _____.
5. An instrument that measures rainfall is a _____.
6. Have your umbrella handy if you are caught in a _____.
7. The _____ led the Indians in a rain dance.
9. A _____ grows in some tropical regions.
10. I'm glad I wore my _____!

ACROSS

1. I can't go to the movie today, but I'll take a _____.
4. A delicious freshwater game fish is the _____.
8. My rubber boots are _____.
11. Will you go with _____ to visit Rainbow Bridge in the state of Utah?
12. Rain is good for plants and good for _____, too!
13. It rained today down by the *dock* -- I almost fell on a slippery _____!
14. A region of little rainfall on a mountain slope is called a _____.

RAINBOW RING-AROUND

Life is much more interesting because of all the marvelous colors that brighten the world. In each section of the rainbow ring-around on the next page, draw 3 things that are that particular color. Color the pictures.

Now make your own rainbow ring-around game to play with a friend. Draw 2 rainbow ring-around circles on construction paper, label each section with a rainbow color, and cut out the circles. To play the game, try to spot one object of each color on the ring-around circle. The object must be in the room you are in! Draw and color the object in the correct space on the circle. (Only when you actually spot an object may you draw and color it!) The first one to complete a ring-around circle wins the game.

Rainbow ring-around is a fun game for the car, too. You might be surprised at how many colors you will notice once you begin playing the game!

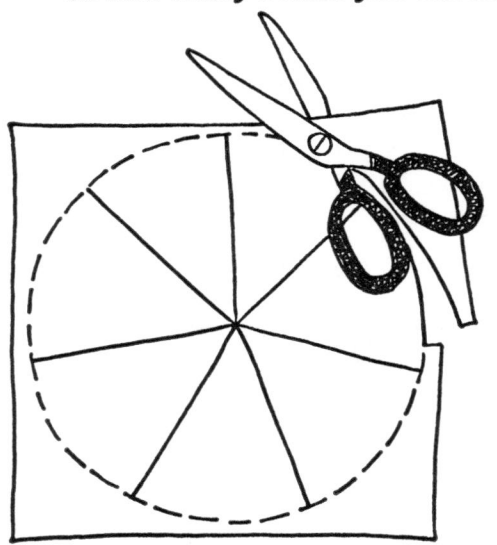

*sometimes a certain saying can give a wrong impression,
such words have hidden meaning -- they're only an expression.*

Draw lines to match each expression on the left with its actual meaning on the right.

It's raining cats and dogs.   Due to rain, the game was postponed.

Save it for a rainy day.   When one unlucky thing happens, it seems that many more unlucky things happen, too.

The game was rained out.   I'd like to do it some other time.

I'll take a rain check.   It's raining very hard!

When it rains, it pours.   Put it away for the future.

Draw a picture to illustrate your favorite "rainbow" expression.

RAINBOW RIDDLES

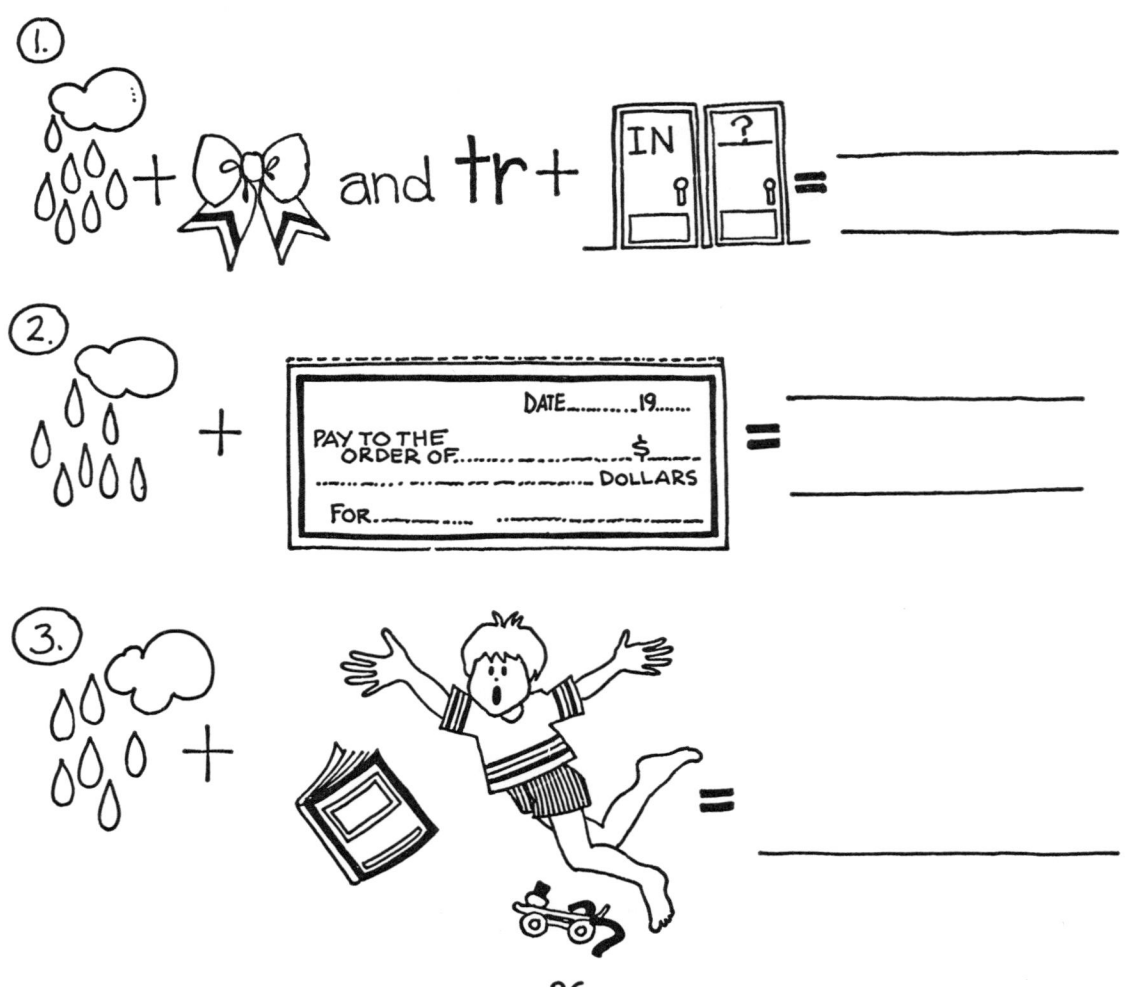

COLOR A TRUE RAINBOW

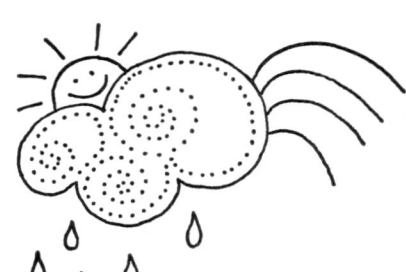

To color a true rainbow, read each sentence below. If the statement is true, color the rainbow band as directed. If the statement is false, do not color the band at all.

1. If a rainbow is caused by the sun shining on raindrops, color the #1 band red.
2. If brown is a color in the rainbow, color the #2 band brown.
3. If the primary colors are red, yellow, and blue, color the #6 band indigo.
4. If raindrops split the sunlight into colors, color the #2 band orange.
5. If mixing red and green makes violet, color the #7 band red.
6. If mixing yellow and blue makes green, color the #4 band green.
7. If scientists have found leprechauns hiding under rainbows, color the #5 band yellow.
8. If you can make a rainbow by standing with your back to the sun and holding a running garden hose in front of you at a 45 degree angle, color the #7 band violet.
9. If you can see a rainbow only after a thundershower, color the #3 band red.
10. If looking through colored objects makes some colors look different, color the #5 band blue.
11. If mixing blue and yellow makes orange, color the #7 band orange.
12. If rainbows can be seen at midnight, color the #3 band orange.
13. If rainbows can be seen in only half of the countries of the world, color the #3 band indigo.
14. If there are 7 colors in the rainbow, color the #3 band yellow.

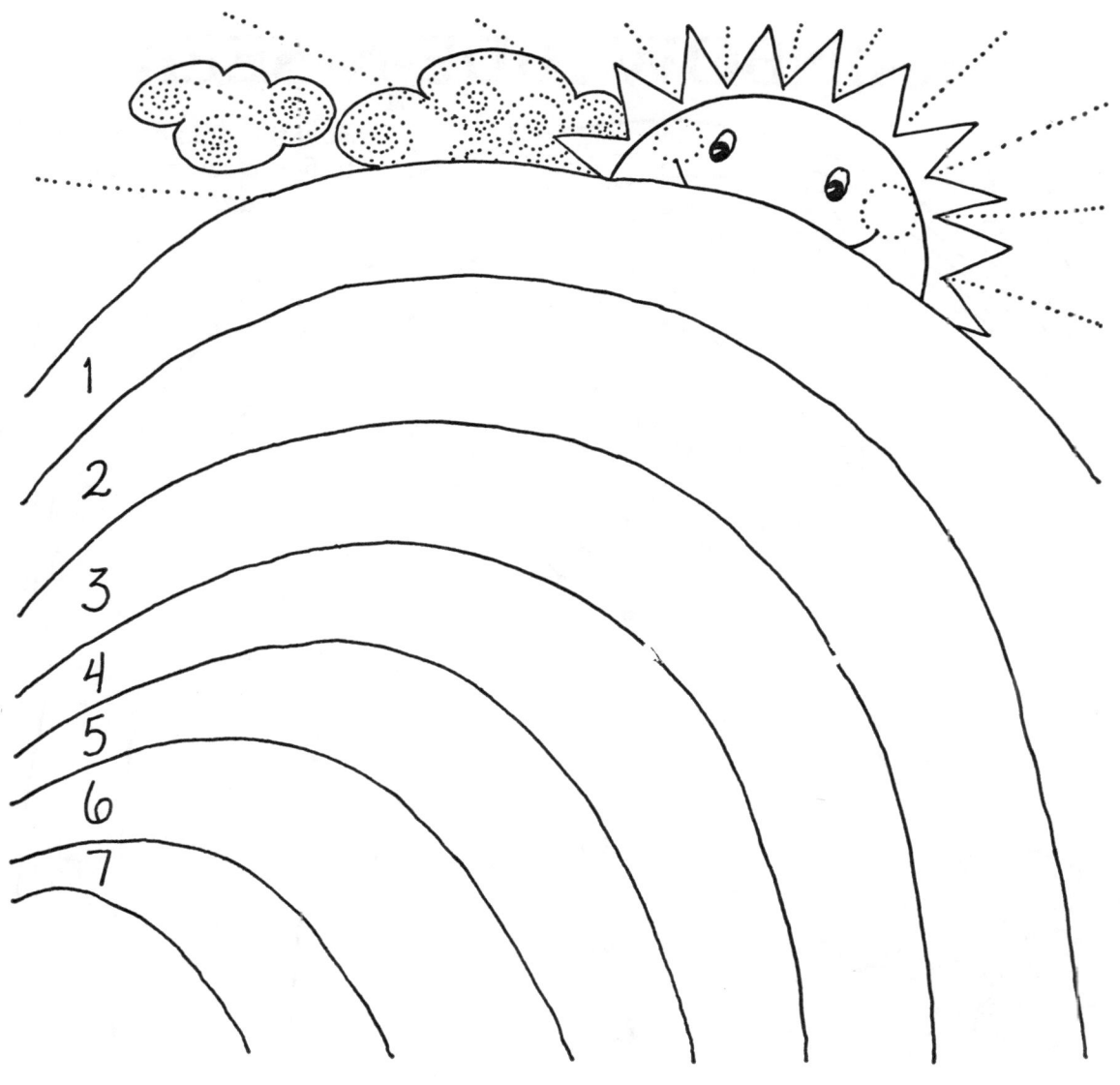

RAINBOW HIDE-N-SEEK

Follow the dots from A to Z to find a rainbow-loving creature!

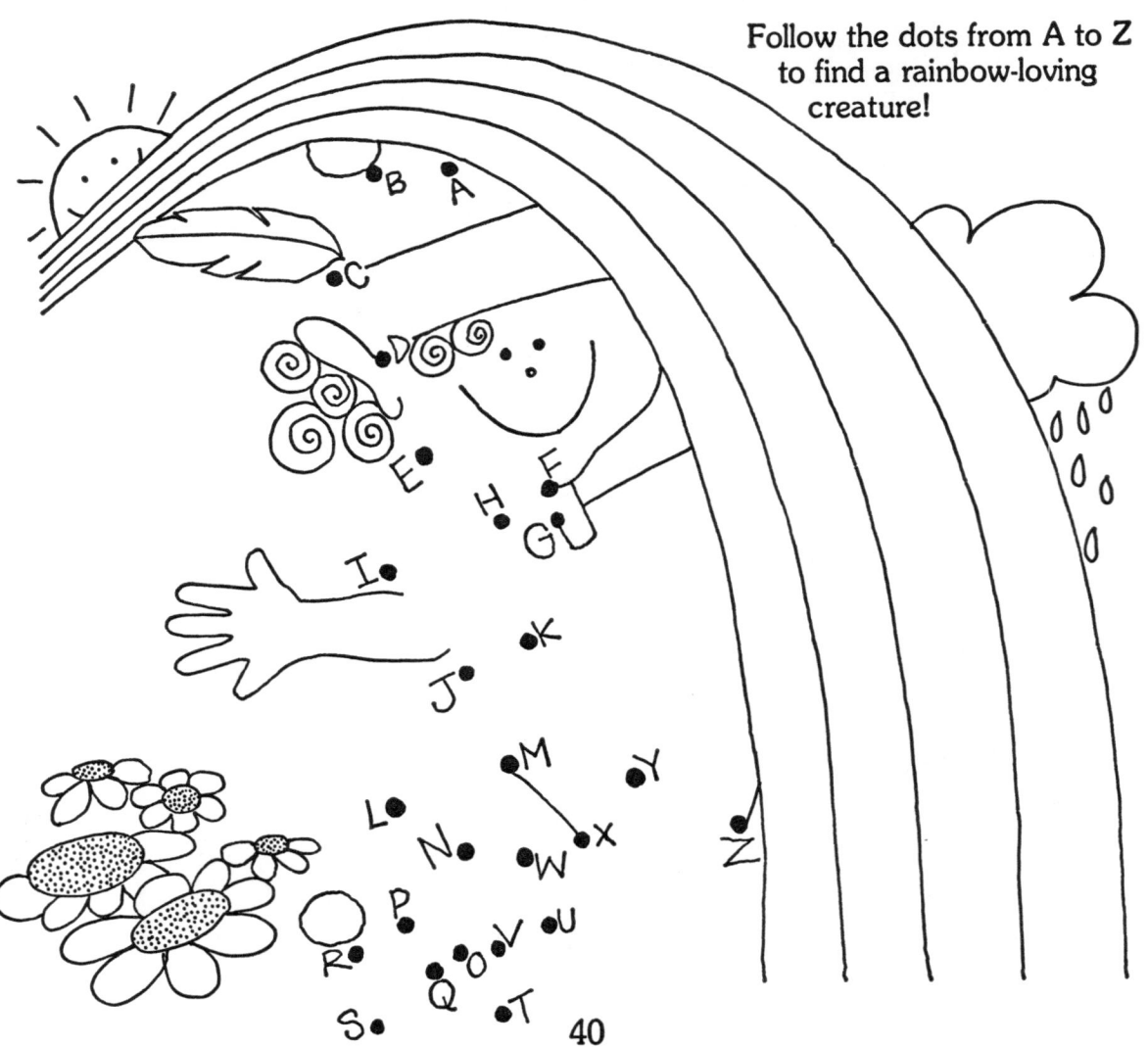

"RAIN BOWS"

*color each bow for lots of fun
and you will make a "rain bow" pun!*

Follow the color guide to color the bows on this page. When you're done, you will have made a "rain bow" pun!

1-red
2-orange
3-yellow
4-green
5-blue
6-indigo (a dark violet-blue)
7-violet (bluish-purple)

SOMEWHERE OVER THE RAINBOW

play this game to find a pot of gold!

WHAT TO USE:
- cardboard box (shirt box size)
- piece of white cardboard or heavy white paper
- markers or crayons
- scissors
- ruler or other straightedge

WHAT TO DO:
1. Draw a rainbow in the bottom of the box. Be sure to include all 7 colors: red, orange, yellow, green, blue, indigo, violet.
2. Label one end of the rainbow "start" and the other end "finish". You may want to draw a pot of gold at the "finish" end of the rainbow.
3. With a dark marker, divide each band of the rainbow into sections. Make as many as you like, but be sure to make an equal number of sections on each band.
4. Use a ruler to draw a grid on the cardboard as shown.
5. Write the numbers 1, 2, and 3 repeatedly on the squares. Write "move back 1 space" on 2 squares.
6. Color 7 squares to match the 7 colors of the rainbow, or write the 7 color words on the squares.

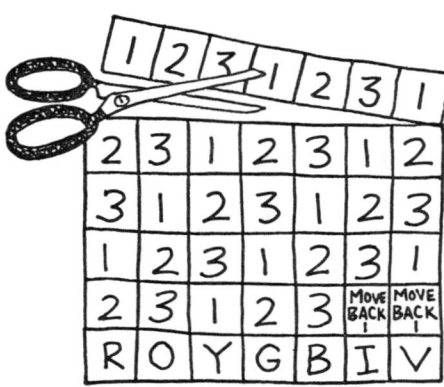

42

7. Cut out all of the squares.
8. Put each of the 7 color squares at the "start" end of the the matching color band. (Each color square represents one player.)
9. Shuffle and stack the other squares, face down.

WHAT IS FUN:
Ask some friends to play this rainbow game with you. (No more than 7 people may play.)

Take turns picking the top card from the stack and moving your color square the designated number of spaces. Return each card to the bottom of the stack. Continue picking cards and moving towards the finish line until someone reaches the pot of gold!

RAINDROP PRISMS

Choose a word from the list below that will fit in each set of blocks and that will make sense with the rest of the sentence. Then, use the first letter of each "block" word to fill in the seven blocks at the end of the story. Unscramble the letters to find out what a raindrop prism makes!

A triangular piece of glass ⬜⬜ called a prism. A prism ⬜⬜⬜⬜⬜ rays of white light that pass through it. The ⬜⬜⬜⬜⬜ light exits the prism in a rainbow colored pattern. The colors of the pattern are always blue-violet at one end and red at the ⬜⬜⬜⬜⬜ end.

After a rainstorm, the raindrops in the ⬜⬜⬜ act like prisms. The ⬜⬜⬜⬜⬜⬜⬜⬜⬜ separate the sunlight into its colored parts. ⬜⬜⬜ you have a beautiful ⬜⬜⬜⬜⬜⬜⬜!

other   raindrops   air
white   bends   now
is

As you can see, the Sun sends it's light through the raindrops to make a rainbow just like white light through a prism.

SOLE-O-RAINBOW

just for you and a friend or two

FIRST: Take off one of your sneakers ...
SECOND: Lightly trace around the sole of the sneaker on a large sheet of white paper.
THIRD: Use markers of rainbow colors to make a rainbow inside the sneaker shape.
FOURTH: Now hang your sole-o-rainbow on your wall to remind you that rainbow makers can find rainbows wherever they go if they'll only look for them!

RAINBOW AWARD

Someone you know deserves a rainbow today -- for having a birthday, for doing a good deed, for making a special accomplishment, or just for being a very special person.

Use your creativity to think of the most clever design possible for a special award. Then, use construction paper and markers to make a rainbow award that you will be proud to present!

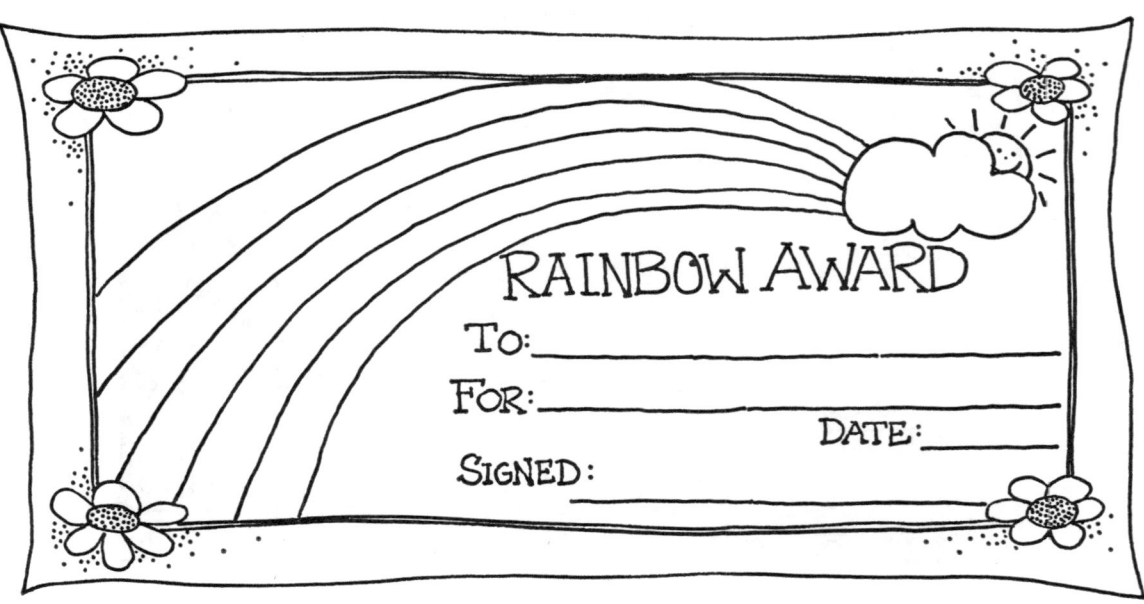

RAINBOW SNEAKERS

*you will feel so neat
with rainbows on your feet!*

WHAT TO USE:
- pair of sneakers
- permanent color markers
- paper
- pencil

WHAT TO DO:
1. Using a pencil, draw a rainbow on each sneaker. Draw lightly so that you may erase if you need to. Work with the drawings until you have 2 rainbows that complement each other.
2. Use the permanent markers to trace and color in the pencil drawings.

SPIN A RAINBOW

*watch the colors mix and blend,
spin a rainbow with a friend!*

WHAT TO USE:
- cardboard
- short pencils
- scissors
- markers or crayons

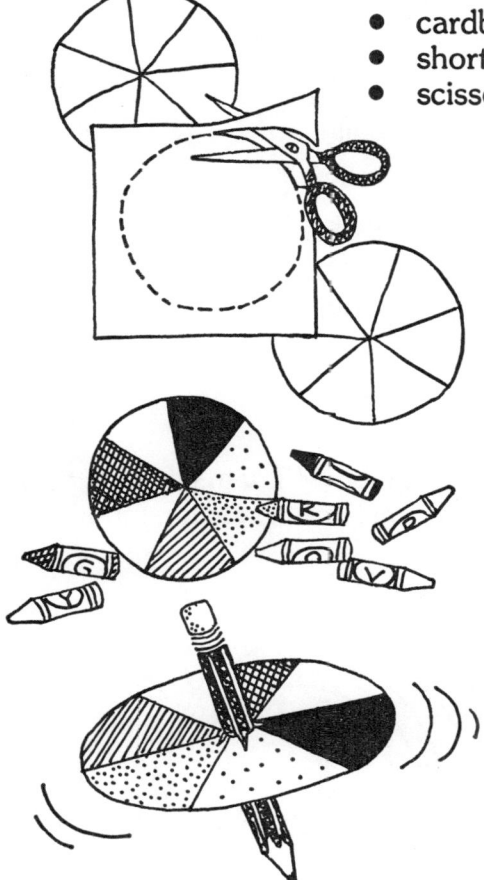

WHAT TO DO:
1. Cut out several circles from cardboard.
2. Draw lines to divide each circle into 7 triangular sections.
3. Color each section one of the 7 rainbow colors.
4. Make a hole in the exact center of each circle and push a pencil through it.
5. Now spin the rainbow circles on the floor or table and watch the colors blend and mix!

WHAT IS FUN:
Following the same directions, make rainbow circles using heavy paper and toothpicks. Number the sections 1-7. Use these rainbow circles instead of dice with a favorite board game. When the circle stops spinning, the number that the pencil is pointing to tells you how many spaces to move.

RAINBOW FRUIT BOWL

Find and circle the names of 7 fruits, one for each color of the rainbow. Write the names beside the colors. Then, use the leftover letters to spell the name of a treat you would like to eat!

_ _ _ _ _ _	red
_ _ _ _ _ _ _	orange
_ _ _ _ _ _	yellow
_ _ _ _ _	green
_ _ _ _ _ _ _ _ _ _ _	blue
_ _ _ _ _	indigo
_ _ _ _ _ _	violet

_ _ _ _ _ _ _ _ _ _ _

Can you name a vegetable for each color of the rainbow? Try making your own word find puzzle with 7 hidden vegetable names, one for each rainbow color, and see if your friends can solve it!

A RAINBOW TO REMEMBER

To sharpen your memory and make a long trip more fun, try playing this recall game.

The key to the game is to listen carefully. The first player begins by saying, "I'm following a rainbow of a very special kind, and when I reach the end I know that I will find...", and then completes the sentence with an object. The second player repeats the sentence and object, and then adds a second object. Each player repeats the sentence and the objects, in the order that each was added, and then adds another object to the list. Keep taking turns. If a player forgets one of the objects in the list, the player is out of the game. The one to stay in the game the longest is the winner.

Start a new round to improve your memory!

HAS ANYBODY SEEN A RAINBOW?

Do a little rainbow research . . .

Ask 10 people you know when they last saw a rainbow. To make your study more scientific, ask people of different ages and with different interests. Ask the people where they were and what time of day it was when they saw the rainbow. Then, ask if they spotted the rainbow themselves or if someone pointed it out to them. Finally, ask if they counted to make sure there were 7 colors. See if they can name the colors of the rainbow.

Make a graph to show your findings. You may be surprised to find out who really sees rainbows.

RAINBOW PENCIL TOPPERS

To turn an ordinary pencil into an extraordinary "rainbow" pencil, trace, color and cut out the rainbows on this page.

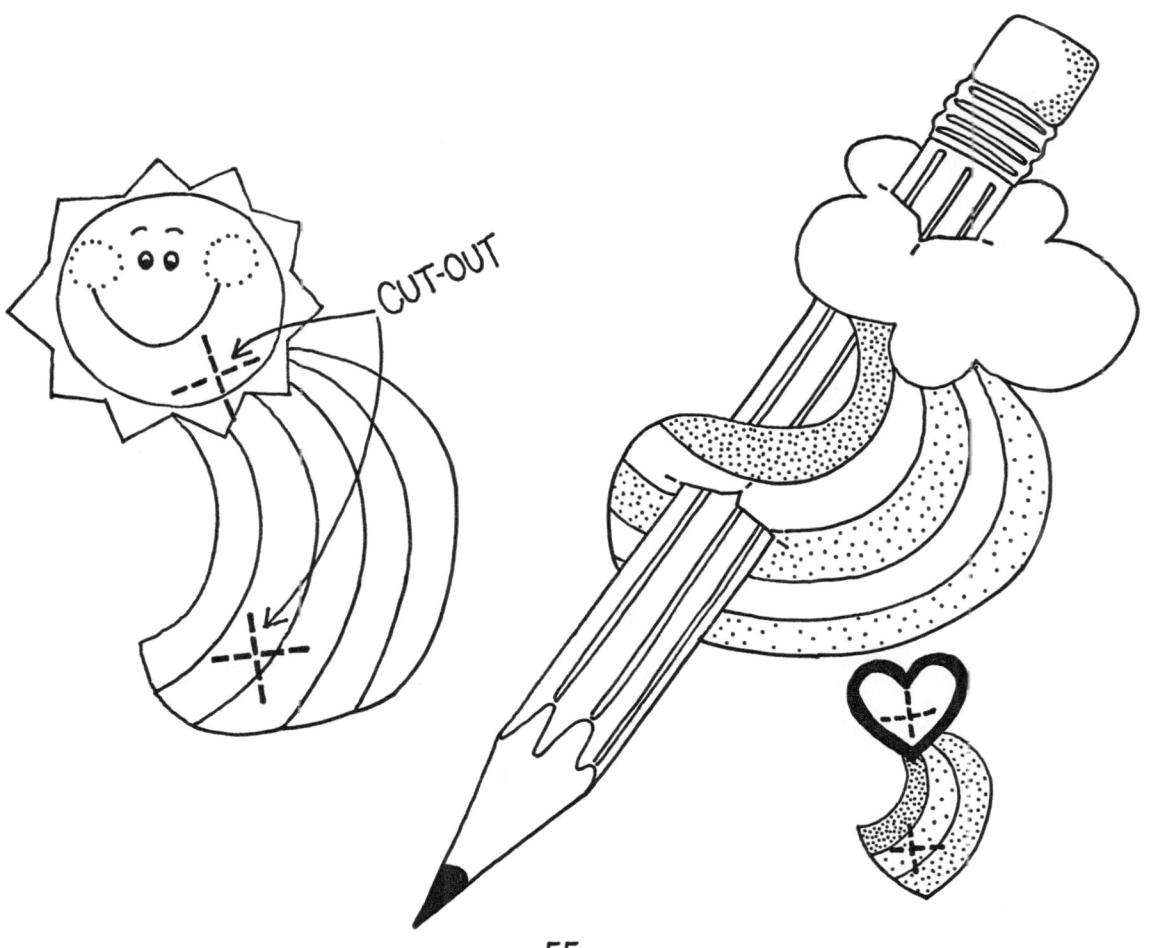

MEET PROFESSOR ROY G. BIV

meet Roy G. Biv, Ph. D--
he's a rainbow authority!

he made this chart for you to see
what fun mixing colors can be!

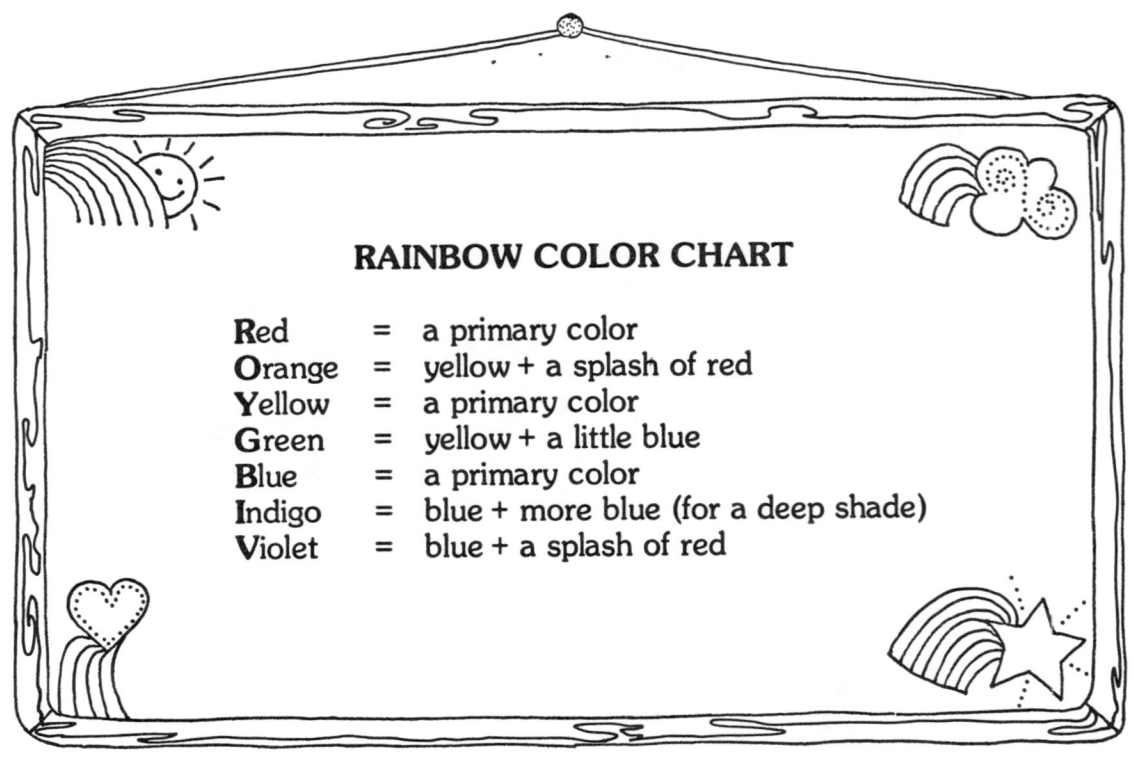

RAINBOW COLOR CHART

Red	=	a primary color
Orange	=	yellow + a splash of red
Yellow	=	a primary color
Green	=	yellow + a little blue
Blue	=	a primary color
Indigo	=	blue + more blue (for a deep shade)
Violet	=	blue + a splash of red

RAINBOW BUBBLES

blow your own rainbows!

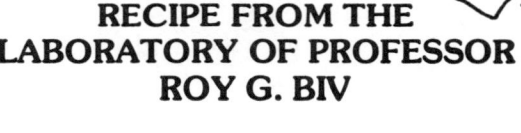

RECIPE FROM THE LABORATORY OF PROFESSOR ROY G. BIV

WHAT TO USE:
- 1 cup water
- ½ teaspoon sugar
- 2 teaspoons liquid detergent
- small container
- drinking straws and/or thread spools

WHAT TO DO:
1. Mix all ingredients in a small container.
2. Dip a straw or thread spool into the liquid mixture. Then, blow through the straw or thread spool to make bubbles.

Blow big bubbles, tiny bubbles, and in-between bubbles. Look for rainbows in every bubble you blow!

DOUGH YOUR OWN RAINBOW

a recipe you may "knead"!

RECIPE FROM THE LABORATORY OF PROFESSOR ROY G. BIV

WHAT TO USE:
- 2 cups self-rising flour
- 2 tablespoons cooking oil
- 2 tablespoons alum
- 7 paper muffin cups
- 2 tablespoons salt
- 1½ cups boiling water
- food coloring (red, yellow, and blue)

WHAT TO DO:
1. Mix all of the ingredients to form a dough. Knead the dough as you would knead cookie dough. (Press and squeeze the dough until it stiffens a little.)
2. Divide the dough into 7 equal parts and put each part in a paper muffin cup.
3. Add drops of food coloring to each cup to make the 7 rainbow colors. (Refer to the color chart on page 58.)
4. Mold each cup of dough into a rainbow-shaped band. Press the 7 bands together to shape a rainbow. Note: This rainbow may not be eaten!

SHAKE A SANDY RAINBOW

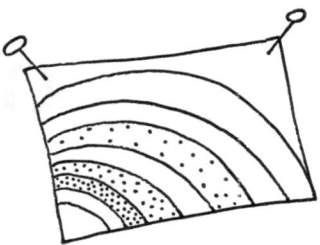

with sand and powdered paint

RECIPE FROM THE LABORATORY OF PROFESSOR ROY G. BIV

WHAT TO USE:
- 2 cups sifted, clean, dry sand
- paintbrush
- water
- glue
- powdered tempera paint (red, yellow, blue)

WHAT TO DO:
1. Divide the sand into equal portions on 7 paper plates.
2. Mix tempera paint with the sand on each plate to make the 7 rainbow colors. (See the color chart on page 58 for mixing colors.)
3. Draw a rainbow on construction paper.
4. Add water to glue to make a very thin paste.
5. Using a paintbrush, spread the thin paste all over the rainbow, being careful to stay within the outline.
6. Gently shake each color of sand, one at a time, onto the rainbow to make the 7 color bands.

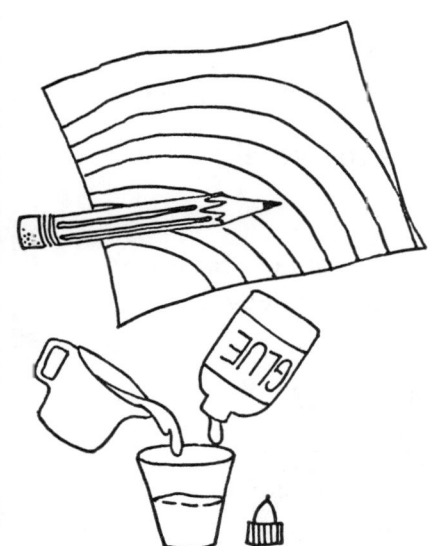

RAINBOW CUBES

RECIPE FROM THE LABORATORY OF PROFESSOR ROY G. BIV

WHAT TO USE:
- ice tray
- food coloring
  (red, yellow, blue)
- water
- spoon

WHAT TO DO:
1. Fill an ice tray with water.
2. Add food coloring to each section of the tray to make the rainbow colors. (See the color chart on page 58.)
3. Put the tray in the freezer and wait for the cubes to freeze!

WHAT IS FUN:
Drop rainbow cubes in a glass of your favorite light-colored punch. Sip away as you watch the frozen rainbow melt right before your very eyes!

RAINBOW REFLECTIONS

create your very own rainbow

WHAT YOU USE:
- pan of water
- mirror

WHAT TO DO:
1. Fill a shallow pan with water and place it on a table next to a sunny window.
2. Hold a mirror at one end of the pan so that the mirror catches the sunlight and reflects it on the wall.
3. Tilt the mirror and shift the pan so that the reflection on the wall breaks into rainbow colors. You may have to work hard to find the right angle, but the beautiful rainbow will make it worth the effort!

WHAT IS FUN:
Make-believe you are a scientist and demonstrate how rainbows are made when water splits sunlight into colors as directed above. Then, stir the water in the pan to make the rainbow disappear! Conclude the demonstration by explaining what causes rainbows to appear in the sky.

RAINBOW POPSICLES

*making rainbow popsicles is really quite a treat --
pour the liquid, let it freeze, and then it's time to eat!*

WHAT TO USE:
- light-colored punch
- food coloring (red, yellow, blue)
- craft sticks
- paper cups

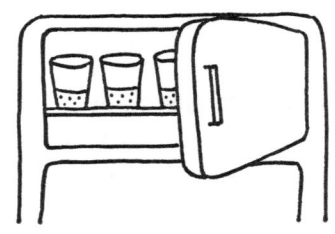

WHAT TO DO:
1. Pour equal amounts of punch into 3 paper cups.
2. Add food coloring to make rainbow colors. (See the color chart on page 58 for mixing colors.)
3. Fill other paper cups, one for each popsicle, 1/3 full with one rainbow color each. Put the cups in the freezer.
4. When the punch is slightly frozen, insert a craft stick into the center of each cup.
5. Pour a second layer in each cup, a different color from the first layer. Return each cup to the freezer.

6. When the second layer is slightly frozen, pour a third layer in each cup, a different color than the other layers. Return each cup to the freezer.

7. Let the popsicles freeze. When you are ready for a treat, take a popsicle from the freezer and peel off the paper cup. (Dip the cup in warm water to loosen it.)

   Note: You might like to make different rainbow treats by adding more layers or by making each popsicle one rainbow color!

WHAT IS FUN:
Share your rainbow treats with friends. Invite your friends to a "rainbow" party and serve each one a rainbow on a stick!

RAINBOW COOKIES

*for a treat that is enticing --
make cookies with rainbow icing!*

WHAT TO USE:
for cookies:
- refrigerated cookie dough (use your favorite recipe!)
- rainbow cookie cutters (or make cardboard patterns by tracing the rainbows on pages 70 and 71)
- flour
- rolling pin
- greased cookie sheet
- knife

for icing:
- 1 cup sifted confectioners' sugar
- ½ teaspoon vanilla
- 1½ teaspoons milk
- food coloring
- paper cups

WHAT TO DO:
1. Flour a cutting surface and roll out the cookie dough.
2. Use cookie cutters or homemade patterns to cut rainbow cookies.
3. Make the icing while the cookies are baking. Mix all the ingredients listed to make the icing.
4. Spoon the icing evenly into paper cups. (Use one cup for each color you want to make.)
5. Add food coloring to the cups to make rainbow colors. (See the color chart on page 58.)
6. After the cookies have cooled, ice them with deliciously beautiful rainbow colors!

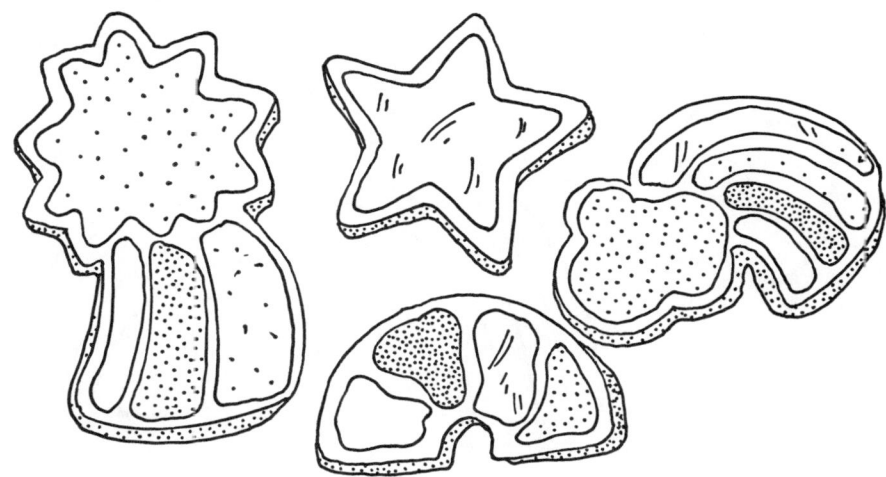

RAINBOW PATTERNS

rainbows, rainbows everywhere -- won't you take a look?
use these rainbows with activities found inside this book.
trace them, color them, cut them out, add glitter, yarn or lace,
they will surely bring a smile to everybody's face

FILE YOUR RAINBOWS

rainbow ideas for anytime!

WHAT TO USE:
- an infant's white shoe box (or box of approximate size)
- markers
- index cards
- cardboard

WHAT TO DO:
1. If there is any writing on the box, cover the box with pastel construction paper.
2. Draw and color a big rainbow on the top and sides of the box.
3. Write "rainbow recipes" on each index card (one for every rainbow project, activity, or game you want to keep on file).
4. Choose headings to help you organize your recipes. Cut out cardboard heading "dividers", each a little "taller" than the index cards.

5. Print each heading at the top of a "divider" card.
6. Arrange the heading cards in the box.
7. File each index card behind the appropriate heading card.

WHAT IS FUN:
Keep a pencil and extra index cards in the box. Look for rainbow games, puzzles and mazes. Try to find directions for things to cook, draw, paint, or sew with rainbows. Flip through magazines and books to find songs, dances and plays about rainbows. Copy the best of the rainbow ideas you find on cards for your box. As you continue to add "rainbow recipes" to your collection, you will never be without a fun project to share with your family, friends, or classmates!

ONE DOZEN AND ONE MAKE-AND-TAKE RAINBOWS

Once you have become a rainbow maker, you and your friends will think of many creative uses for your rainbow recipes and patterns. For starters, try some of these.

1. Make rainbow party invitations! Fold a piece of paper and draw one half of a rainbow, with the highest point starting at the fold. Cut out the rainbow, decorate the outside, and write the invitation on the inside.

2. Make a rainbow mobile. Cut out rainbows from construction paper or cardboard and hang them from a tree branch or coat hanger with strong thread.

3. Make rainbow stencils to use in designing original stationery or greeting cards.

4. Make open-faced sandwiches by spreading rainbow-colored cream cheese on bread.

5. Paint rainbows on sponges or potatoes and make rainbow prints to decorate gift wrap.

6. Cut out and color cardboard rainbows to hang on a Christmas tree.

7. Cut out, color, and glue together cardboard rainbows to make a wreath for your front door.

8. Make a rainbow tote by painting a soft drink carton with blue tempera paint and decorating it with lots of paper rainbows.

9. Decorate brown lunch bags with rainbows to make lunch time more fun. Draw, color or paste rainbows on the bags. A set of 5 different rainbow lunch bags, one for each day of the week, would make a great gift for someone who takes a lunch to work or school!

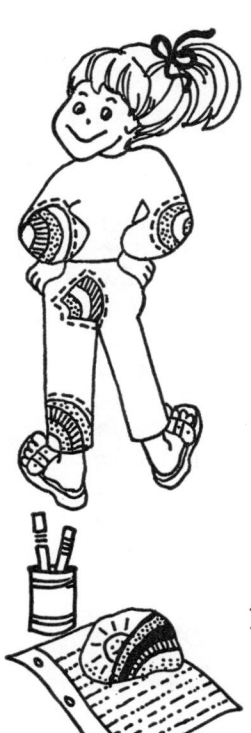

10. Patch a pair of jeans, a sweater, or a T-shirt with rainbows cut from fabric scraps.

11. Make a small rainbow bean bag by stitching two rainbow fabric scraps together and stuffing beans inside.

12. Paint a rainbow on a smooth rock to make a paperweight for your desk.

13. Finger paint a rainbow with soap suds. Combine one cup of liquid soap and 2 tablespoons of liquid starch. Beat the mixture until it thickens. Pour the liquid equally into 7 paper cups. Add food coloring to make the 7 colors of the rainbow. Paint a sudsy rainbow!

ANSWER KEY

Pages 36 & 37

1. Rainbow Trout
2. Rain Check
3. Rainfall
4. Raincoat
5. Rainproof
6. Rain Forest

Page 38

1. true
2. false
3. true
4. true
5. false
6. true
7. false
8. true
9. false
10. true
11. false
12. false
13. false
14. true

RAINDROP PRISMS

Choose a word from the list below that will fit in each set of blocks and that will make sense with the rest of the sentence. Then, use the first letter of each "block" word to fill in the seven blocks at the end of the story. Unscramble the letters to find out what a raindrop prism makes!

A triangular piece of glass `IS` called a prism. A prism `BENDS` rays of white light that pass through it. The `WHITE` light exits the prism in a rainbow colored pattern. The colors of the pattern are always blue-violet at one end and red at the `OTHER` end.

After a rainstorm, the raindrops in the `AIR` act like prisms. The `RAINDROPS` separate the sunlight into its colored parts. `NOW` you have a beautiful `RAINBOW`!

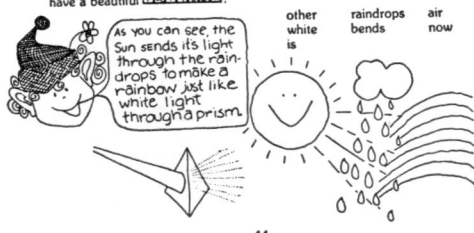

other raindrops air
white bends now
is

RAINBOW FRUIT BOWL

Find and circle the names of 7 fruits, one for each color of the rainbow. Write the names beside the colors. Then, use the leftover letters to spell the name of a treat you would like to eat!

Apple — red
Orange — orange
Lemon — yellow
Lime — green
Blueberries — blue
Plum — indigo
Grape — violet

Fruit Salad

Can you name a vegetable for each color of the rainbow? Try making your own word find puzzle with 7 hidden vegetable names, one for each rainbow color, and see if your friends can solve it!

INDEX

A
awards, 46-47

B
bean bag, 77
bookmarks, 26
bubbles, 60

C
candles, 14-15
candy, 21
color charts, 58-59
cookies, 68-69
crossword, 30-31

D
dot-to-dot, 40
dough rainbow, 61

E
expressions, 34

F
file box, 72-73
frozen punch cubes, 64

G
games, 32-33, 42-43, 49, 52-53

I
ice cubes, 64

L
lunch bags, 76

M
milk carton, 14-15
mobile, 74
molding dough, 61
music, 24-25

P
painting, 12-13, 16-17, 24-25, 62-63
paperweight, 77
party invitations, 74
patterns, 70-71
pencil toppers, 55
place mats, 18
plastic bags, 22-23
popsicles, 66-67
prisms, 44
puzzles, 30-31, 38-39, 40, 44, 50-51

R
rainbow
  patches, 77
  prints, 75
  research, 54
  sandwiches, 75
  survey, 54
  tote, 76
rainwear, 22-23
riddles, 36-37

S
sand rainbow, 62-63
sneakers, 45, 43
spinning top, 49
stencils, 74
string container, 19

T
tree ornaments, 75
true/false, 38-39

W
word choice, 44
word find, 50-51
wreath, 76